Watch It Grow

Watch an Oak Tree Grow

by Kirsten Chang

Bullfrog Books

Ideas for Parents and Teachers

Bullfrog Books let children practice reading informational text at the earliest reading levels. Repetition, familiar words, and photo labels support early readers.

Before Reading
- Discuss the cover photo. What does it tell them?
- Look at the picture glossary together. Read and discuss the words.

Read the Book
- "Walk" through the book and look at the photos. Let the child ask questions. Point out the photo labels.
- Read the book to the child, or have him or her read independently.

After Reading
- Prompt the child to think more. Ask: Have you seen an oak tree? Can you explain how they grow?

Bullfrog Books are published by Jump!
5357 Penn Avenue South
Minneapolis, MN 55419
www.jumplibrary.com

Library of Congress Cataloging-in-Publication Data

Names: Chang, Kirsten, author.
Title: Watch an oak tree grow / by Kirsten Chang.
Description: Minneapolis, MN: Jump!, Inc., [2019]
Series: Watch it grow | Audience: Age 5–8.
Audience: K to Grade 3. | Includes index.
Identifiers: LCCN 2018023996 (print)
LCCN 2018024723 (ebook)
ISBN 9781641282727 (ebook)
ISBN 9781641282703 (hardcover: alk. paper)
ISBN 9781641282710 (paperback)
Subjects: LCSH: Oak—Growth—Juvenile literature.
Classification: LCC SB413.O34 (ebook) | LCC SB413.
O34 C43 2019 (print) | DDC 634.9/721—dc23
LC record available at https://lccn.loc.gov/2018023996

Editor: Jenna Trnka
Designer: Michelle Sonnek

Photo Credits: sandr/Shutterstock, cover; Zerbor/Shutterstock, 1; Fotofermer/Shutterstock, 3; Destiny13/Shutterstock, 4; Tatyana Mi/Shutterstock, 5; Photo Fun/Shutterstock, 6–7, 22ml; Dieter Zinsser/Shutterstock, 8, 22t; Viktor_Kitaykin/iStock, 9 (acorn), 23tl; Anton-Burakov/Shutterstock, 9 (soil), 23tl, 23br; Michael P Gadomski/Getty, 10–11, 22mr, 23bl, 23tr; jurgal/Shutterstock, 12–13, 22br; basel101658/Shutterstock, 14–15, 22bl; somchaij/Shutterstock, 16; Ollinka/Shutterstock, 17; PFlemingWeb/Shutterstock, 18–19; Emilian Danaila/Shutterstock, 20–21; Aigars Jukna/Shutterstock, 24.

Printed in the United States of America at Corporate Graphics in North Mankato, Minnesota.

Table of Contents

A Tall Tree

There is an oak tree in the park.

It is tall!

How does an
oak tree grow?

acorn

It starts as an acorn.

An acorn is a nut.

It grows on
an oak tree.

It is green.

In fall, it turns brown.

It falls from the tree.
It lands on rich soil.

A root grows
in the soil.

It needs water.

In a few months,
a shoot grows.

shoot

root

Leaves grow from
the shoot.

The leaves get sun.

The plant turns
sunlight into food.

It grows bigger.

It takes years to become a tree.

The tree
needs water.

It needs sunlight.

An oak tree can
grow 80 feet
(24 meters) tall!

After 20 years, the tree grows acorns.

More trees will grow.

Life Cycle of an Oak Tree

How does an oak tree grow?

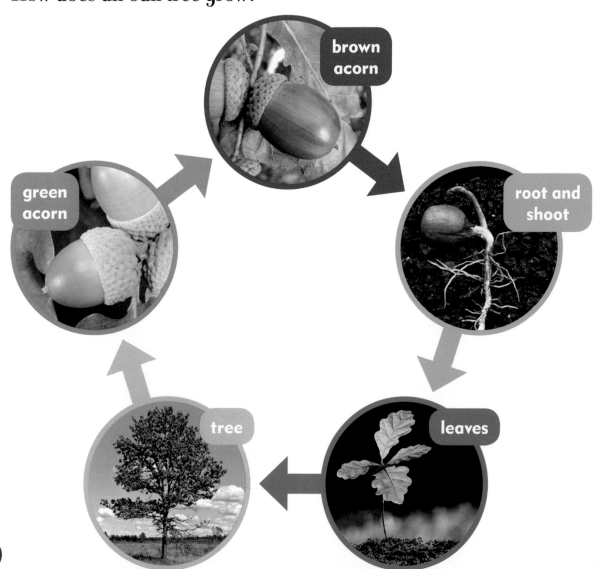

brown acorn

green acorn

root and shoot

leaves

tree

Picture Glossary

rich
Productive, fertile; rich soil is good for growing plants.

root
Part of a plant that grows underground and gets water and food from the soil.

shoot
A plant stem.

soil
Another word for dirt.

Index

To Learn More

Learning more is as easy as 1, 2, 3.

1) Go to www.factsurfer.com

2) Enter "watchanoaktreegrow" into the search box.

3) Click the "Surf" button to see a list of websites.

With factsurfer.com, finding more information is just a click away.